A VOICE FOR THE CHILDREN IN THE BACK ROW

A VOICE FOR THE CHILDREN IN THE BACK ROW

Kathleen Robinson

To order additional copies of this book, contact:
Xlibris Corporation
1-888-795-4274
www.Xlibris.com
Orders@Xlibris.com
112554

This book is dedicated to James, an educator, par excellence who encouraged me to relate the stories on behalf of all the marginalized students.

Contents

A Voice For The Children In The Back Row

The children who sit at the back of the class probably do so for any of three main reasons: (1) They are tall and for practical purposes go there voluntarily or are placed there by the teacher. (2) They are shy or lacking confidence and believe that they are less likely to have questions directed at them there. (3) They desire undisturbed freedom from the teacher—they form friendships where talking or surreptitious eating becomes a preferred activity, or they are the class bullies.

Some teachers readily detect these escape mechanisms and make every effort to ensure that no child is deprived of the requisite attention, while others simply limit their focus to those children who demonstrate the greatest willingness to learn. The children at the back of the class are often the ones with psychological scars and, if left unattended, further develop more scars of emotional neglect. In this narrative, the voice relates the story—in distinct episodes—of four different children, each within an almost ten-year span encountered along the pathway of pedagogical development.

The intention is simply to reinforce a connectivity among practicing teachers who continue to reach out to students that may otherwise be inadvertently overlooked despite the former's training in pedagogy. After a few years, even the most dedicated practitioners experience occasional burnout or wash out. The author hopes that the real-life episodes contained herein will touch the hearts of such practitioners by rekindling the sparks they felt when they first walked down the aisle in graduation regalia, vowing to others and to themselves to make a difference.

The voice speaks variously through a graduate pupil-teacher during the period of the 1950s-1960s, an elementary teacher during the 1970s-1980s, and two secondary school teachers during the 1990s-2000s. Each episodic illumination juxtaposes the parapsychological situation of a particular child to a distinctive historical epoch anecdotally told of a fanciful paradise place in our global village. Teachers recall many stories, sometimes quite identical; therefore, the voice takes no responsibility for any peculiar resemblance to persons known to the readers.

CAPSULE I

THE CHILD IN THE BACK ROW

Children go to school and learn well.
> *—"Dan Is the Man in the Van" sung by*
> *Slinger Francisco (Popular calypsonian,1963)*

"There is ah brown gyul in the ring, tralalala, and she looks like ah sugar and ah plum, plum. Girl show me your motion, tralalala . . ."

That was her final year, 1959, in our school; she had blossomed and was now bravely showing her motion in the ring.

She was sent to the back of the class where there was room. The next term, in her new class, she chose the back seat. She had entered school during that last term—April to July 1956—the beginning of her new term did not reflect much change. I had assisted her former teacher and then I was on my own with the same students who were promoted.

She would play with friends from the higher class. She seemed happy then, laughing and screaming as she ran around playing catch. Closer observations revealed sad eyes which invariably seemed to focus on some distant object: her daydreaming. She could not understand much of what was taking place in the class because she was so often in that trance.

How best could I help her to touch base with the reality of her present environment? What did she not like about being in class? What was it she loved so much about the outdoors? Was it a simple case of confinement versus freedom? I questioned myself. Those eyes revealed a story that I needed to relate to the world because there were many others like her; there were so many "little broken hearts" desperately pleading for repair.

EPISODE I

NEGOTIATING
THE SECURITY FENCES

Her name is Ixora—a beautiful tropical flower traditionally used as fencing that, though not much in demand, blooms year-round and lends beauty to a well-structured home. Just as her namesake, she was beautiful in many special ways; the eponymously named Ixora smiled as I requested space at her desk. I enquired whether she understood the fractions that I had just explained. She whispered affirmatively. However, in her book, she had begun an incorrect approach.

"No, no, do not add the denominators. We must have a common factor—that is what I meant when I said the lowest common factor (LCM). OK, focus now . . ."

I slowly explained each step, peering into her eyes to read her comprehension.

She smiled; she had understood. I made the big red tick that all the children passionately loved and instructed her to continue using the method in solving the other problems.

After that day, Ixora began to come to my desk early on mornings before the other children had arrived; when they came, she would quietly disappear. Having observed this pattern three times in one week, I waited for her to duck among the other children, trying to disappear. I placed my hand on her shoulder, drew her to me, and held her in a gentle embrace. I asked the others, "Do you all like Ixora's curls?" They affirmed that they did, and two of them commented that most times her hair was combed in curls. She had the attention of her peers and she looked completely contented, although shyly accepting the remarks with an attractive smile that revealed even white teeth.

I tried my best to make Ixora a part of my class. I sought to interrupt her perpetual reveries. She remained extremely happy and uninhibited when outdoors with her friends whom I soon learnt were, in fact, her cousins. Yet they were all of different ethnicities. Two of them looked to be pure East Indians, one of mixed Caucasian, while the fourth had features that were either Carib or strongly tinged with Chinese. Ixora herself was mixed, apparently 'dougla' or 'doula' the derogatory Hindi term, which is a mix of Indian and African. I later learnt that she was mixed with Spanish and African, a rather typical result of the miscegenation inherent in Caribee society: the family represented a kaleidoscope of races.

Ixora shared her secrets with me. Gradually, I began to understand her sad eyes, her reason for dreaming. There was a chasm in her little heart; at eight years old, it was too much for her. Slowly, it eroded her power of concentration, but I battled to win her trust that would enable her to face the challenges of mathematics and biology. She was proficient at the creative arts—her mother once told me that she would often find her hiding under the bed or in the outdoor lavatory, sitting on the covered seat reading with the lights of a flambeau when she should be engaged in some assigned chore.

One day, Ixora stared at me for a long while before stating softly, "I miss my daddy."

"Why?" I stupidly asked.

Of course, I wasn't aware of it, but it should not have surprised me. About four other students in the class also belonged to single-parent homes. Moreover, I knew of five others whose parents remained together only out of strict adherence to churchly tenets or commitment to their children's welfare. Those children were equally affected.

"He did not move up north with us," she guardedly responded.

"Oh!" I said, as if in a daze, not wanting to betray any sign of surprise.

"I miss my teacher too."

"Really?" I looked her in the eye. "What was her name?" I asked, trying to encourage conversation.

"Mrs. Royce, and she was nice, I love my teacher. Ma said one day we will go to look for her."

"And you really miss your daddy too?" I tried to redirect her focus to the main object of my concern.

"Yep!" she responded as the bell rang. I saw in her eyes her eagerness to join her cousins outside.

I studied her back as she ran outside. My heart bled for Ixora. She was extremely quiet, very soft-spoken, and shy. I saw her climbing the slide and laughing as she slid down and ran around the rung to climb up again. Play was her therapy, playing and reading. I wondered about her father and about the many parents who break marriage vows when there are children involved. I felt burdened whenever I recalled her sad, dreamy eyes. Awareness of her story unwittingly made me resolve to keep my charges happy once they were in my class. I pledged to shorten the days of unhappiness for all my Ixoras.

My former mentor had warned me about becoming too entangled in my students' affairs; he had advised me to be strict. I could not help myself; I was a young graduate of the pupil-teacher system and I possessed almost the same energy level as my students.

Ixora often drifted away during mathematics and biology—those were not her favourite subjects. However, I got her undivided attention during reading, comprehension, spelling, creative writing, and art. Often, she would draw a picture of a house with a dog at the door. One day, she informed me that the house had been her house in south and the dog was her dog that she had left behind. She added that it had taken him "four whole months" to find them in the north. I told her that was impossible, but she insisted that she saw him all dirty and thin, and when she called his name, he came to her. He followed her home so she and her siblings fed and bathed the dog. Then for the first time, she raised her voice commandingly, "It is my dog from the south!"

I smiled and said OK, feeling a bit ruffled by her unexpectedly aggressive tone.

I contemplated her story about the dog; seemingly, many others had also doubted that the dog was originally from her home in the south, but she refused to admit that it was not the same dog. It was a part of what she had in the south. If I were to befriend her, I had to leave her with her belief. I needed to get her on my side so that her pain would abate and she could excel to the best of her potential.

That child was different from the other children in my class. As was previously mentioned, some of them had come from dysfunctional homes, they were weak, but nonetheless happy in and out of the classroom. That child, Ixora, was generally melancholy, only perking up when I gave her my attention. She remained aloof with the others and unwilling to make friends. Her friends were her cousins. The family was evidently a close-knit one.

EPISODE 2

VENTURING DEEPER
INTO THE PSYCHE

One cold, rainy October morning, some children came running on to the school compound. One of them was her cousin—the little part-Caucasian girl with long brown curls. I called her and she obediently came. "Yes, miss."

"You are Ixora's cousin, what is your name?"

"Yeah, I am Paula."

"Where is she?"

"She home, she gets sick when it rains, so her ma says no school for her."

"OK, tell her I asked for her. Is she coughing?"

"No, but when she gets wet, she always coughs and gets fever."

"All right . . . . does she live at your house?" Shrewdly, I began to probe her; I really wanted to get into Ixora's psyche.

"No, she lives in my other aunt's house because it's bigger."

"Oh, she does not live with her mother."

"Kinda, her mother and brother live by Gramma. When her ma is not there, she must go by Aunty. Aunty has more room, sometimes I sleep there too."

"Does she like to go by this Aunty?"

"No, she cries every evening and every morning, but just now when Aunty's tenants leave, her ma will rent that house. They will live next to us."

"Are you happy about that?" I knew she would be, her entire face lit up with the thought.

"Yep! I used to live by them in the south. She is my bestest cousin."

Aha! I thought, that was the reason she always ran to that cousin's class when the bell rang. She was holding on to everything she still had from the south. South, this child grieved for all that was in the south. My conversation with her cousin Paula had revealed a lot. Ixora did not miss anything new as my class attendance was quite low that day.

The next day dawned bright—all my students were there. Ixora had come to class early as usual, carrying a handful of Buttercup flowers for my desk. I enquired whether her cousin told her that I had asked for her. She responded positively with a smile and informed me that she could not allow her head or feet to get wet. She went on to explain that once she had almost died on account of a high fever, so she could never get those parts of her body wet unless she was bathing. She showed me the pair of socks and crepsoles (sneakers) in her bag in case her feet got wet.

I asked who took care of her when she fell ill. She said her mother, but continued to relate that should she fall ill, it would be really hard for her mother because then she would not be able to go to work. She insisted that her mother needed to get money to rent a house so that her brother who lived far could live with them, and they would all sleep and wake in the same house. I felt like crying. What a burden to try to remain healthy so that one's mother would not need to take time off the job to take care of a child. I enquired about her mother's job, thinking that she was perhaps a maid, only to be told that she worked at one of the large chain stores where she was a bilingual sales clerk, speaking Spanish and English.

I asked about her brothers. She explained that her baby brother stayed with her mother at her grandmother's home, but her other brother "stayed far, far, and he visited every weekend". I encouraged her to reminisce about her happiest times that she confessed were, of course, on weekends when everybody stayed by her grandmother. They slept on the floor, but when she awoke on Saturday mornings, her grandmother would already have bake and hot dark chocolate 'tea' prepared for them. On Sunday mornings, they all went to church and had a happy time until afternoon when her brother had to be taken back to the far, far place. When her mother returned, she then had to leave for her aunty's place to sleep.

Dysfunction was a novelty to this child—six months after the split—she and her siblings had to "face a different music" on mornings and evenings. I wondered about her brother who was completely alienated each week. Ixora, at least, enjoyed daily interactions with her mother. She had been so grounded in the nuclear family environment that she could scarcely adapt to the sudden change to an extended family setting with her brother being placed in another extended setting, detached from her own. As the other students came towards my desk, Ixora placed a finger on her lips. I smiled conspiratorially, acknowledging that I would keep the secret. She ran off, perhaps to her cousin Paula. I knew she now trusted me; she had revealed some treasured family secrets.

Slowly, I recognized that the exuberance she displayed on Fridays was in anticipation of the weekend gatherings. One Friday, I remarked that she must be very happy as she would be seeing her brother the following day. She excitedly told me that her brother would be moving to her grandmother's home and would not be returning to their aunt's home as he was being badly treated there. That was another secret because only her grandparents, her mother, and she were privy to that plan. I made a gleeful noise and hugged her. Indeed, I had been chosen to share the secrets of the family.

I placed her in the middle row of the class and assigned a taller child to the seat she previously occupied. She was not keen, but I insisted. Slowly, she began showing more interest in biology and mathematics. Although she remained amongst the weaker students, her term marks had improved slightly. Her marks in other areas were invariably 70 percent and above. She indicated that her mother was not pleased with her report. Her mother had threatened that if she got those marks again, she would send her to "cook in the white people's kitchen". Her mother had told her that her only hope lay in her books.

I felt this sounded like harsh advice, but recognized that black children, as exhorted in song by the young popular calypsonian, had to be aware of the impossibility of ever getting a good job without having a sound education: "Children go to school and learn well; otherwise, later on in life, you go ketch real hell." I had two more terms to help her improve so that she could escape the ignominy of life as a maid. Her mother had further insisted that black people could only achieve full freedom if they studied hard. I understood her mother's words only too well. Ixora was the darkest complexioned in her family and was frequently reminded of it; that was most likely the reason for such warnings.

I was introduced to her charming dad on one of his infrequent visits to the school. Ixora proudly said to him, "This is my best teacher!" He chatted amiably with me about her and then she took him to her cousins. Paula in particular hugged him affectionately.

After he left the school, Ixora's happiness turned to gloom. Any attempt to hug her would cause the tears to flow, so I left her alone to daydream and to control her teary eyes. I found myself wishing I had the moral authority to instruct her father not to visit his daughter at school since it was impossible to recapture her interest after his visits. I had only managed to tell him that she seemed to miss him greatly to which he dryly replied,

"I know." I showed him her sketches of her house and her dog, making enquiries at the same time about the dog. He confirmed that the dog had run away about the second week after they left the home; he was aware that she had found a dog almost like hers, Scott, but which he had not seen because he did not visit the home. He too believed that it was impossible for a dog to walk that far, but felt she would eventually get over it. *Indeed, I thought, just like she must get over the happiness her parents have denied her.*

At the end of that academic year, I felt like I had buffered much of her pain. I had given her one more adult to trust in a place away from home. Her progress in her weak areas was not remarkable, due in part to insufficient practice, but she kept trying and that was worth more than simply giving up. There were now as many smiles in the classroom as there were out of it.

Her father's career was a respectable one in the country's military service, and he apparently had provided all that he possibly could for his family within the nuclear setting. In fact, the parents had even been able to take care of another child from the extended family. Ixora's new challenge was adjusting to life within an extended family household. Her mother persistently complained that she had to provide for all her children's needs on a meager salary since the court had stipulated a mere $8 monthly maintenance allowance per child. She, like many other single mothers, was certainly required to perform something akin to a mini miracle to fulfill the needs of her children. She appeared resolute, and that, I felt, was a prerequisite for Ixora maintaining good academic discipline.

EPISODE 3

TAKING ROOT IN AN ECLECTIC GARDEN

Many interesting things were happening in the colonial twin islands of Caribee and Cruso during the post-World War II period. Several events directly influenced young educators and students. I was no exception.

I began teaching at age fourteen through the pupil-teacher monitoring system and eventually became a qualified primary school teacher. At the time, many Africans and East Indians, incapable of accessing university education, opted for this course as a means of ascending the social ladder. Like me, they were selected and placed under the tutelage of a mentor. Several brilliant locals were granted scholarships to go to England, the mother country, to study law, medicine, and philosophy. Others, through the aegis of the Presbyterian missionaries—then actively proselytizing among the East Indians in Caribee—were afforded the opportunity to study in Canada. In 1932, Lall Ramkes became, in this way, the first Caribeean of East Indian descent to obtain a degree. Ustace Hyarima who, in 1945, had received his doctorate in philosophy and history from Cambridge had, by 1955, returned to commit all his dedication among the people of Caribee and Cruso. This small-statured mixed African man who humbly lectured to the public in the main city square on evenings became Caribee and Cruso first premier and prime minister in 1956 and 1962 respectively. I count myself among the many families and educators on whom his influence had a positive impact.

A teacher's salary was small, but the profession was well respected in the community. We stood up for what we believed to be right. As a Roman Catholic, I was employed in a Roman Catholic school and lived in accordance with the tenets of my faith. We, the faithful, felt a sense of religious pride as the church was a powerful institution and we were the beneficiaries of certain privileges. There were also attendant obligations. As a case in point, unmarried female Roman Catholic teachers who became pregnant while on the job were invariably posted to remote schools and obliged to remain there until the birth of the child, which was kept quite secret until marriage. I was instilled with firm belief in the sanctity of the institution of marriage, hence my enduring empathy with my suffering students from broken homes.

Ixora's class had been my first. I first noticed Ixora who had been registered midway during the previous school's term. She was Roman Catholic, and the Roman Catholic Church always helped the faithful who were active financial members; she would otherwise have had to wait until the beginning of the new school year or seek admission to the nearby government school since the compulsory age for attendance was five to twelve. However, no good Catholic families sent their offspring to the government schools. Ixora's family members were regular churchgoers: the grandfather was a fairly independent cocoa-panyol (fair Spanish) farmer whose first son owned a well-established business in the capital. They were well-known to the parish priest and that favoured an out-of-season admittance for Ixora.

Ixora was determined to succeed because she did not want to work in the "white people's kitchen". At that time, many discussions about black pride and intellectual development were being broached by the newly elected premier, Ustace Hyarima. Ixora's mother frequently cited excerpts from these speeches to remind her daughter what she needed to do to elevate herself.

Colonial society was stratified primarily along lines of race and class. Racially, there was further subdivision corresponding to gradations of complexion. The lighter complexioned Afro-Caribeean and Crusonian was more highly regarded than the darker one. A similar practice existed among the East Indians who seemingly adopted a vestigial caste system where Brahmins consisted of, for the most part, the lightly complexioned priests while the Dravidians, their more duskily complexioned compatriots, generally assumed the roles of servants or lower castes (untouchables) within the system.

With respect to class and class consciousness, the class system essentially operated in accordance with some confluence between the financial worth of a family and its physiological and geological proximity to the dominant European phenotype. Generally, Caucasians were considered to be the superior class, but among themselves, those of greatest rank were those who laid claim to established lineage and property ownership. The Chinese presence was in the main unobtrusive, constituting a largely insulated community enjoying primarily functional links with the rest of the society. They had arrived before the East Indians, but their light complexion ensured that those who chose to remain, quickly gravitated away from unskilled plantation labour to opportunities in business and commerce. That was the socioeconomic and cultural reality of our society in the late 1950s to early 1960s, but we abided in peace. That, at least, was how I perceived it as a young pupil-teacher on the threshold of my career.

In my view, Ustace Hyarima played a critical role in fostering racial tolerance by exhorting us to desist from use of the derogatory terms, *nigger* and *coolie*. Perhaps it took a while, but eventually, B*lack* and *Indian* became a more natural part of the vernacular. I still think of him as the quintessential teacher of the nation. As a nation, we, particularly those of us of African descent, felt a deep sense of pride in his achievements. He was truly loved by many because of his charisma and his insistence on providing free universal secondary education, a radical philosophy at the time. He emphasized that the future investment was in the schooling of the nation's children. Many parents such as Ixora's mother hammered that idea into their children's head. In addition, many of those parents began to educate themselves in the community centres that offered adult instruction in crafts, drama, and music. Academic knowledge was the domain of the teachers who helped as much as possible to make scholars of our charges by preparing them for success in the Caribee and Cruso College Exhibition Examination and, by extension, for free secondary education. Ustace Hyarima proposed free secondary education for all from 1960, disregarding the intention of his predecessor, Alberto Goma, to increase placement through the College Exhibitions. However, there were glitches, and free education for all took several years to become a reality. Those who were not successful at the College Exhibition either paid for secondary education or were apprenticed to successful tradesmen or artisans.

Ixora was not fortunate to procure free secondary schooling, but her mother sent her to a private secondary school. Throughout her primary schooling, she remained close to me, regaling me each morning with gifts of seasonal fruits. She remained basically shy around adults but blended well with other children in her class. She visited me towards the end of each term during her first year at high school.

There were several others from broken homes whom I embraced, but none like my first, Ixora who would often seat herself in the back row. When I got married, I moved to my husband's village. Ixora, like several others, never failed to send me a Christmas card each year. The number of cards has been reduced including Ixora's, but wherever she is, I know that I had touched her life positively. That is what matters.

Suggested Further Readings:

John-Charles-Baynes, S. (2009, March). *The school climate and its impact upon the self-concept of adolescents in the secondary school system and its relationship to academic achievers.* Paper presented at the Tenth SALISES Annual Conference on School Climate and Impact, UWI Cave Hill Campus, Barbados. Abstract retrieved from http://www.cavehill.UWI.edu/salises/conf

Ministry of Education, Trinidad and Tobago. (1993). *Education policy paper (1993-2003): National Task Force of Education (white paper)—Philosophy and educational objectives.* Port of Spain, Republic of Trinidad and Tobago: Ministry of Education.

Pukey, W. W. (1970). *Self-concept and school achievement.* Upper Saddle River, NJ: Prentice Hall.

Tyson, E. (2012). *Progress in politics: Progress in education?* Retrieved from http://Jamaica-gleaner.com/gleaner/20120101/cleisure/cleisure/s.html

CAPSULE II

1970

I am young, gifted and black.
—originally sung by Nina Simone (1970)

I stood at my desk, totally embarrassed, as the most unforgettable child in my Standard 5 class walked to his seat at the back of the class. He had been a student in my class from September 1969 to March 1970 and it had begun with utter torment for me. Never did I believe that I could harbor feelings of animosity towards a child, but for six months, I absolutely abhorred this boy. Much later in my career, I realized in retrospect that I had failed to treat him with the respect he genuinely deserved.

EPISODE I

UPSIDE-DOWN EMBARRASSMENT

ANOTHER CHILD IN THE BACK ROW

His name was John. I had just finished an explanation of compound interest. Some students did not fully understand it, so I decided to have John come to the board to explain the formulae. He had been sitting at the back, evidently distracted by a cube with which he was playing. It occurred to me to have all the distracted ones come to the board and publicly embarrass themselves as a sort of punishment for not paying attention.

He walked slowly to the board, took the stick of chalk from my outstretched hand, and began slowly explaining each step, asking as he looked around, "Everyone understands?" The children's response at the end of each step was a resounding and enthusiastic "Yeah!"

At the end of his explanation, he flashed a broad smile and he said, "Proven! There is no need to continue!" He handed me the chalk and jauntily walked to his seat at the back of the class. I made no comment. I was embarrassed.

The child had indeed done a better job than I. I felt like I was being taught how to teach. I detested that! I hated him at that moment. He, indisputably, was the enemy.

Each time I looked at John, he appeared to be scoffing at my incompetence in mathematics. I took special care in preparing my math lessons, simply because I had in the past experienced difficulties in the area. Teaching at the Standard 5 level didn't pose a real challenge for me; once my textbook was opened, I could glance at the worked examples and I felt completely in charge.

It had been my second year teaching at that level, and I rather enjoyed it because from March to July, with exams over, the work at school became light. I indulged my students in craft, physical education, and board games—a deserved reward after all the hard work. The previous year, 8 percent of my students had passed for prestige schools, 42 percent for grammar schools, and the rest who had failed went their separate ways either to private schools or trade schools depending on their parents' inclination and financial status. I felt my class would not do as well in 1970 because efficiently, effectively, a ten-year-old student had deflated my ego. He had tossed me into a state of perpetual mental turmoil.

That child would either stare at me, waiting to openly correct my errors, or yawn silently—I, in turn, was always spying on him; his undisturbed yawn and snide smirk—indeed, he was never outwardly disrespectful. Towards the end of the year, the more I reflected, the more I saw that I and not the child was the one with the problem.

Once, during the monthly Parents and Teachers Association's meeting, his parents came to address me concerning John. I observed that they were quite surprised by my comments—rude, difficult to speak to, nonparticipating, and sometimes talkative. The mother indicated that they spoke about school regularly and he had never expressed any adverse feelings, except that he felt bored, something she had grown accustomed to as he had said that of each class. When asked to give an example of his rudeness, all I could manage was 'yawning and laughing during class'; of course, his laugh was that smirk I sometimes saw on his face. Really, the child could have been half smiling at anything but me. The parents were not surprised. Instead, their expression betrayed a bland "So what!"

I noted that, intellectually, the child was above the level of his peers, and I could make no claim for having raised him to that level. His oral and written language skills, mathematics, science, and social studies were all superior. Once, when I began a lesson on "The Family", he raised his hands, and I, thinking he was about to pose a question directly related to the lesson, allowed him. Instead, he stood up to expand upon the extended family in polygamous relationships, and in response to his easy conversational style, the children clamoured to hear more. I menacingly told them that was not part of the syllabus and demanded that he sit and follow the outline in the text. I detected the smirk, the ever-present half-smile as he obediently moved to comply. He never seemed to be easily flustered. He sat and looked through the window as if amused at something in the distance. I detested that about him too. Why didn't he cry or try to be openly rude? I never got the upper hand with him so I abhorred him.

EPISODE 2

STUDENT REVOLUTIONARY

February 3, 1970: A large crowd of boys assembled on the lower compound of the school's playground. John sat on the stump of a large mango tree that had recently been felled and left to add to the ambiance of the schoolyard. Around him, some boys were seated on their school bags, some standing, all eagerly listening as he explained all about the demands of Daano to the Prime Minister, Ustace Hyarima. I listened intently too. Fear gripped me. I was allowing him to 'teach' again. Few of the boys had observed me, but I was obviously oblivious to them all. I powerfully clapped my hands and authoritatively demanded everyone go to his class. I saw some hateful stares. I heard as if in a whisper, "house nigger!"

I shouted, "Who said that?"

In unison, a few of them responded, "Said what?"

Not desirous of making a fool of myself, I continued to insist that they all go to their classes. In fact, twenty minutes still remained before the bell should ring for class; they were well within their rights. *That damn boy!* I silently thought.

It was the first time that he appeared annoyed as he looked at his watch and then at me. He had no smirk, just an unusual question in his eyes. My heart sunk for an unknown reason. I feared that at any moment I would see the leader of the Black Power Revolutionaries at the classroom door. Only then, did I think that he too must have been seeing my hate and was prepared to reciprocate with silent disgust. I felt that I got into his head, but I could not feel victorious. He still seemed to be ahead of me. *Why?*

At the end of the day and for the first time since that September morning when I had called him to the board, I felt unashamedly empowered by my behavior because of the entire class' reaction. They were humbled into silence, even John looked like a loser in a battle. He was quiet, passive, yet recalcitrant in his new submissive attitude. Everyone was quiet; I knew, quietly angry, I needed them in that mode. During the lunch session, he was at it again, they had a "watch out"—two of them were facing the direction where any teacher could be seen approaching. When the bell rang, they immediately returned to their classes. The silence in my class was deafening, but I did not care—I had renewed authority—it was a powerful day for me.

When my husband came home, he was relieved to see me in such a pleasant mood. I told him my story as I usually did on evenings; we had a good laugh at John and the other children. But my joy was short-lived when I took out the *Evening News* from my husband's briefcase.

I was not shocked at the front-page article of an intended march from Central Caribee to the main city in the north. I was, however, stunned to see a picture of John's father in an African outfit, his head tied with a red ribbon and his clenched fist in the air, as he stood within a group of well-known Black Power agitators. He was described as a lecturer from the University of Caribee and Cruso. I was then deeply concerned about his son's meeting with the boys. I felt that I had to talk to the principal the next day about that boy, John who was negatively influencing his peers. My moment of glory had completely faded as I felt overly anxious about the next school day.

EPISODE 3

A HISTORY LESSON

I entered the principal's office to sign the register and to seek an appointed time to discuss the matter concerning John. As I bent to sign the register that was on the principal's desk, his presence hit me like a cold iron slab. I did not sign, I stood up straight, my jaws unnoticeably dropped, then I realized the principal had told me to have a seat—the only vacant chair next to the father. The principal had called the first senior teacher to keep the register and to close the door.

The principal smiled as he introduced me and informed me that the matter concerned John, the gentleman's son. The father was truly a gentleman—soft-spoken, smiling, and gesticulating from wrist to palms as he commented on the injustice of my demands to the children who were only inquisitive about the current situation. He insisted that I should not stunt critical learning. My defense seemed to have blown into thin air. He explained the purpose of the Black Power Movement as it pertained to education—a curriculum that was outdated and not meeting the needs of modern Caribee and Cruso, particularly in the secondary schools where my students would go the following year.

He spoke of the poor economic policies that had affected the entire nation in terms of unemployment and desired remuneration of those employed. When I told him about the racism that had been separating Indians and Africans, he simply smiled. He convincingly continued that it had been the local whites who had been trying to maintain a division and that Indians and blacks had been united against the hiring practices of the white businessmen. I denied that because I believed the Indians had taken no part in the struggle. He named about three of them who had spoken at meetings and intended to march, and he had persuasively commented that many would join when they understood the benefits for the oppressed classes.

A meeting that I felt would be hostile to me ended up being a history lesson for both the principal and me. We rarely spoke about John, and I was happy about that as I felt that I had only then understood the child. The father had told me that he believed that his son could be a challenge in the average class, but there were no special schools for gifted children, and he felt that he needed him to have his feet on the ground and not his nose in the air; hence, he had chosen our school as we generally did quite well at the CCCEE. The principal had explained that he was honoured, while my hurt ego inwardly whispered that the principal should try to teach John. I smiled beyond my hidden pain, shook the father's hand, and departed to sign the register.

All thoughts silently raced through my mind at lightning speed—*he's a professor at the university . . . he is not one of those hoity-toity . . . he does not want his son to be like that either . . . he must be just plain cheap . . . no, he had donated all the trophies and had contributed large sums during our fundraiser . . . he had kept that deceptive smile on his face . . . he had gently touched my shoulders to emphasize a point . . . perhaps he was probably attempting to flirt with me, . . . he is a womanizer . . . black pride, my foot . . . damn child just like him.*

"Oh!" I yelled out—I was just being ridiculous, but at the time, my feelings were very real. I had never bothered about this black consciousness, but the professor touched something in me. I must confess, I took pride in my spiced colour, my almost white kinky-haired husband, and clearly my handsome fair son. I felt we were not disturbed by the rumblings of Black Power!

That evening, my husband calmly stated, "One drop of black blood means we are black. You know my grandmother is as black as night and I love her and she loves me dearly! My mother is mixed Caucasian, and I love her just as much." He said no more; he took his *Evening News* and began to read. He too must have felt that conscious awareness of that Daano's message and the unrest in the USA that he had closely followed on the radio.

I had begun to intently listen to the news. I attended meetings that were held in the nearby park. I had been finally convinced that Hyarima was not doing enough for the nation. Empty talk by this once beloved man and glaring corruption had made even Hyarima himself shudder, although he publicly defended one of the main corruption culprits at the time.

I clearly understood the reasoning of John's father. After Caribee and Cruso Common Entrance Examination (CCCEE), I had begun to wear a red wristband, and whenever I greeted certain people, I would raise my fist in the air. That had been my way of showing solidarity with the anti-colonial leaders and the disadvantaged black youths. Kwame Ture, Angela Davis, the Black Panthers, Martin Luther King, Malcolm X—all historically shook America in their quest for social justice. In Caribee, we felt we too had to topple the government of CC or force them to implement proper policies. 'Power to the People of Caribee and Cruso' was a serious mantra.

EPISODE 4

NEUTRALIZING MY FEELINGS

After that meeting with John's father, I slowly begun to understand John, but had not been prepared to show him the warmth that had been replacing the coldness I had felt a few days before. The class continued with its deafening silence when I was in the classroom or generally in their presence. I no longer enjoyed that authority. I wished to ask John to tell me what he knew, but I just could not give him that power—he had held it silently for six months.

I checked many books on gifted children. Nothing was offered in Caribee and Cruso for children like that. I felt sorry for him because I realized that teachers like me were only impeding such student's progress. I enquired of his previous teachers how they had treated his exceptional knowledge and they too said, "Just ignore him, he will pass the exam any way!" That certainly was not fair. I had started to look at him differently. I longed to show him that respect that I had slowly developed for his father and for him too, but I had a great fear of losing my autonomy.

Slowly, I observed a change in his attitude to me. His eyes did not seem to be questioning me, rather I perceived an understanding. His smile was genuinely directed at me. Once, he came up to the board and whispered, "Miss, you erroneously placed the *e* before *i* in the word *chevalier*." He walked away before he could have heard my soft response, "Thank you." I bit my lip, but I smiled as I corrected the word—*French*, I thought. We had come a long way. I felt we had begun to silently read each other's behaviour. Perhaps he had seen my changed heart through my eyes.

John was sent away for a month immediately after the exams. He returned two weeks prior to the results of the CCCEE. My arms were open for him before he actually reached me. I embraced him tightly, saying at the same time, "I missed you, we all missed you!" That day was all about John and his holiday to Canada.

My class saw the lighter side of me—we had lots of craft, physical exercise, sports—they particularly enjoyed football, cricket and athletics—field trips, drama, literature, and our new language learning skills of Spanish in order to get them ready for secondary school. Before the end of the term, we had a graduation ceremony. Then the results came two weeks later. Only 4 percent of my boys passed for the most prestigious college of Caribee and Cruso—John and his good friend. Twenty percent passed for grammar school and the others failed. My class was the *A* group. The *B* group did much better. That academic year was truly depressing and it truly reflected my results. My friend Joan who had taught John the previous year commented, "See, we told you so, the bright ones always pass!" I reflected, *no matter where they are seated, to be gifted is a privilege of God.*

EPISODE 5

VALEDICTORIAN

At the end of John's Secondary Exam—CCGCE (Caribee and Cruso General Certificate Examination) and Cambridge Advanced Level, he was awarded a scholarship. He was so much taller than his father. He stood almost seven feet, fully developed but gentle as a dove. He moved on to study orthodontics.

At the primary school level, he was the valedictorian. He humourously allegorized teeth in the mouth as children in a classroom. He emphasized that the care which must be taken in the classroom is a serious task for teachers or else children, like teeth, would decay and must be extracted before affecting the entire mouth. At his age, such comments were surprising, but his parents seriously insisted that they did not help him to write anything.

My heart had melted with love and pride for John. I strongly believe that I had learnt from John more than he had learnt from me. The lesson I had learnt had helped me throughout my career: I knew I was a better teacher because of John.

Suggested Further Readings:

Campbell, C. (1997). *Endless education: Main currents in the education system of modern Trinidad and Tobago 1939-1986*. Cave Hill, Barbados: University of the West Indies Press.

Carmichael, S., & Hamilton, C. (1967). *Black power: The politics of liberation in America*. New York, NY: Random House.

CAPSULE III

1990

None but ourselves could free our minds.

—Robert "Bob" Marley (1979)

"Who is it?"

No response.

I moved away from the window, but the pounding on the gate persisted.

"What do you want?"

"Ah could get ah shoes and shirt?"

"Go next door!"

"Yuh eh know me?"

"Wha!"

I will never forget that voice. He came calling that night in November towards the end of the school's term preceding the Christmas holidays of 1993.

He must have been a casualty of the 1990 uprising. Many hearts were either cracked or broken that year. Many of the affected students smiled and continued to laugh at their circumstances, opting to see the lighter side of their sordid situations as they bore the values of the home to the school. At our school on the outskirts of the city, many boys related personal stories of looting: toting refrigerators and stoves on their backs, up the hills to their homes. The mood that September proved rather unsettling as many households had been affected. Many students posed as zealous combatants: Muslims and non-Muslims easily chanted, "Allah O Akbar!" as a means of unsettling the oppressors of the day.

Unable to decipher the full ramifications of their philosophy, they perceived society as *them* versus *us*. Jihad was destined to overthrow the oppressive regime of the day. They deified the Robin Hood who had appointed himself as liberator. The society was fractured, and at that school, the dominant patterns of students' behaviour were clear indicators for all who had eyes to see and ears to hear. Teachers, in stoic silence, continued to teach against the tide of a new militancy.

EPISODE I

Who?

He was a pleasant young man in my Form 4 and later Form 5 class. I always made time to listen to him and to provide any additional assistance he requested. He sat at the back of the class and was often busy trying to complete some assignment that should have been done at home. Akeem had his moods; he did not join in the looting, but his family life was fractured that very July. During his darker moods, he would shut out all sound and motion, but he was never disrespectful to any of his teachers and, in lighter moments, was known to share a good joke and join in the ensuing laughter.

Sometimes, I found it necessary to impound the object of his distraction—invariably, a book in which he would be doing some other teachers' assignment—several other students may have shown their anger in an aggressive manner. He was never unduly ruffled by this action and would immediately thereafter attempt to pay due attention. I would always return the confiscated item before leaving the classroom. After several such encounters, he got the message that I required his undivided attention, as did many of the others. In spite of his social baggage, he gradually improved and was fairly well-prepared for the regional examination in my subject. His good friend Savita assisted where and when she could. She was genuinely concerned about his welfare; she knew so much about his family and understood the challenges he faced.

Akeem lived with his paternal grandparents. His mother had migrated the day of the uprising, July 27, 1990, but he would only say that no one had heard from her for a long time. His father lived somewhere in Caribee, but whenever he came around, he would quarrel with his mother—Akeem's grandmother—that would leave Akeem so incensed that he would think of hurting his father when he became strong enough.

Akeem was a tall athletic-looking young man. He was loving and thoughtful, qualities discernible in the way he thought of his grandmother, although she would often disappoint him by drinking herself into a drunken stupor. He complained about not liking her getting drunk because then he would hear her arguing with his grandfather until he (Akeem) fell asleep. His life was perforated with a yearning for affection, with pain, hunger, and—between the anguish of the once maternal barrel—spent love. I showed him that I cared, occasionally supplementing his meals, but that could only fill a space for a brief period of time in a growing teenager.

I felt that I could work with Akeem during the vacation. There is no code of ethics debarring such assistance in Caribee and Cruso. Akeem came to my home one day without any books. I sternly enquired about his negligence. He smilingly responded that he was not in the mood to study but still felt the need to come. He was having problems related to the dysfunctional situation at home. He, smiling as usual, stated that he wanted to run away. I looked at his glary eyes and plastered smile for a quick second and immediately discouraged such thoughts. I chatted with him about future goals as a strategy for taking his mind off the plethora of problems inundating him. He left me with a smile and a promise that he would try to do some work during the vacation. I gave him my telephone number so he could call if he needed assistance. He never did request any help. He felt as hopeless as most of his peers about his academic future, believing at the time, that the rich would remain rich while the poor received nothing, not even the welfare hustle that they had enjoyed under the previous government.

The new term commenced and progressed in much the same vein. I listened, I offered him words of comfort, I contributed meals when requested, and I hoped that he would achieve some measure of success. July 27, 1990, remained etched in his memory—not the occurrence and after effects of the uprising, but the final breakup of his family, albeit simultaneous with the wider societal breakdown. He was not coping well with a grandmother who loved him dearly but whose vision was often blurred by alcohol. I was always stunned to hear Akeem relate how he would have to wrestle with her to get the bottle out of her hands before emptying its contents in the backyard. At fifteen, Akeem was compelled to make the decisions of a man. That force, that sudden change from living in a home with both parents to surviving in another dysfunctional setting was pervasive; it raped him of his childhood and plunged him violently into manhood.

Akeem's examination results were almost good—threes, the lowest passing grade and fours, failing just under the lowest passing grade—with a bit more diligence, he would have possibly attained better grades. There was every probability of success if he opted to repeat the examination, but he did not care to continue school.

EPISODE 2

DRIVING TO INDEPENDENCE

My car was at the mechanic shop. I had to take a taxi to school. I hailed and entered a PH vehicle (private car offered for hire) and requested that I be dropped off at the school.

"Sure, miss!"

Our eyes met in the rearview mirror. "A-kee-m!" I loudly proclaimed to the astonishment of the other passengers as we smiled.

He asked my permission to go off route to drop another passenger. I consented, realising that he wished to chat privately. And so, he begun telling me of his quest for independence and how he came to acquire the vehicle. Once we got to the school gate, I offered him the fare. He responded, "No, miss. Once you have to take taxi, you can look out for me."

I protested that I would not, if he did not take the fare.

He responded, "Miss, you looked out for me. You tried to help me. I would never forget that. This is the least I could do to show my appreciation."

I reluctantly returned the money to my purse. I advised him that his present job should be considered purely as a temporary means of survival as he could certainly improve himself like Savita and Michael, his buddies. Without looking at me, he emptily promised that he would; he could not look at me. I enquired about his home situation to which he retorted, "Same never ending story, I just keep to myself."

I agreed that that was the wisest option; life could only improve. I reminisced about all the students of Akeem's class until the bell rang. Then, I searched the faces of the present batch—some showed evidence of hidden pain—but I no longer felt any desire to get close to them. My energy was depleted, but each year, one or two would absolutely demand attention—not verbally, but by insistently intruding into my space—over the ensuing years, there would be many more Akeems, but never another as special.

EPISODE 3

A VOICE IN THE WILDERNESS

The voice continued to trouble me. Nothing could quell my unease. I remained convinced that I knew that vagrant's voice. After I had instructed him to go next door, he had turned south of my gate and slowly walked away. *How eerie,* I thought at the time. I felt that he had singled me out, hoping that I would come to the gate so he could attack me. But when I sat at my table, his haunting voice came to me again.

"Yuh eh know me? Me? Me?"

My sons felt I had made the correct decision; I would usually take items to the gate for anyone who called for help. In this case because of the time of night, I refused. Still I could do nothing to dispel the frequent flashback of "Yuh eh know me?" The faceless voice echoed over and over for several weeks, disturbing my equilibrium. I knew the voice was familiar, but I could attach it neither to a face nor a name.

Jogging around the park one evening, I met Savita. I would have continued on my way, but she stopped me.

Breathing heavily, I enquired about her life. She happily told me she was in her first year at UCC. We both rejoiced, then I enquired about Akeem. She seemed surprised that I was unaware he had died some weeks before. She explained that he had lived a life of vagrancy for a short while before his lifeless body had been found.

"Vagrancy! Vagrancy! He came to me", I cried to her. "He came to my gate! He said that he had one side of slipper and wanted a pair of shoes. He also asked for a shirt. He was wearing a vest . . ."

We hugged while she consoled me, saying I would not have recognized him even during the day. I wished her well and bolted to my car, to my home. I was deflated! How had I not recognized Akeem's voice? How could I not recognize a familiar voice crying out in moments of utter despair? My tears are still on the edge whenever I think of Akeem. Sometimes I pondered, . . . *you walked from far to beseech the only one you felt would have helped . . . you got no help . . . you were sent to another . . . but you had too much pride . . . you walked away . . . more hurt . . . she did not acknowledge you! You must be in heaven now, having suffered so much on earth.*

Suggested Further Readings:

Pantin, R. A. (2007). *Days of wrath: The 1990 coup in Trinidad and Tobago.* Lincoln, NE: iUniverse Inc.

Payne, R. K. (2005). *A framework for understanding poverty.* Highlands, TX: aha!Process, Inc.

CAPSULE IV

2003

I would be nothing without you.

—as sung by Bette Midler (1983)

We all seemed to jump at the same time. I had run out of the classroom following the shouts of name-calling and the obvious body music. Nary a sound escaped the teenager as she cowered in a corner of the last classroom.

EPISODE I

THE GAME

"No, miss, no," I beseeched as I got between them, while I too blocked cuffs. Other teachers had run up the steps as they also heard the commotion. They ordered my students back into the classroom. The portly lady had come to my class quite calmly, seeking permission to speak to Victoria. The language she subsequently belched out was unbecoming of one so sartorially outfitted, but nothing surprised us in that school. The school is situated on the easterly outskirts of the city and not much good was matched against it. At best, it was known as the Football School.

The scene that afternoon was certainly a body game of sorts. When the lady had finally settled her frame into the chair drawn for her by the Koko School supervisor, the battered victim sat close to me as if pleading silently for protection. The lady carried on concerning the whimpering girl whom she described as an animal. As she gushed a never-ending stream of demeaning adjectives, the supervisor instructed the student to return to class. That brought an abrupt end to the flow of abusive language.

After being introduced to me by the supervisor, she proceeded to relate her tale of woe, this time in almost hushed tones. The young lady was her protégée. She had taken her off the streets and had vowed to the Lord that she would "raise her up" in the proper way. The girl's father had murdered a neighbour and her mother committed suicide. Her brother was unable to take care of her. She had been living on the streets for sometime before the goodly lady had found her and taken pity on her.

The lady took her time to dress from head to toe as she told us in order to maintain a level head, but at the sight of Victoria, all hell broke loose and that is what we had just witnessed. It seemed to her that Victoria loved to "play games" with her. Instead of using the bathroom, she would select some corner of the house and defecate or urinate in it. The lady's nostrils would often lead her to the unsightly mess. After being flogged as punishment, Victoria would simply target another corner and repeat the process. Therefore, the lady alluded to her as an animal—an undisciplined dog—as she repeatedly called her. I advised the goodly lady that it was futile flogging her as she had developed the habit of casual defecation and urination while living on the streets. If instead, she repeatedly insisted that she clean it herself, perhaps she would stop such behaviour outside the bathroom. The lady stared at me as though I were a genuine Martian.

In the classroom, Victoria was seated at the back of the class with her head on the desk. I went to her, gently patted her head which she raised and looked at me through eyes swollen by the earlier punches. Her lips had grown even thicker; she looked so battered and helpless. The other students were moved to show empathy rather than the usual vicious teenage ridicule although they had overheard some of the unusual testimony of the lady. I gave her some tissue and advised her to rest; she could complete the assignment at home.

After class, the teachers met with the supervisor. We insisted that such an incident should never be allowed to recur. He concurred and immediately issued a directive that all parents/visitors should first report to him and then be accompanied to the student. An unspoken game had begun; Victoria would become our protégée once she was inside the school compound.

Victoria could read, she could orally analyze and comprehend what she had read, but she encountered problems presenting her responses in writing. I resolved to intensify literacy strategies for Victoria. The art teacher, as if reading my thoughts, indicated that she would help her to express herself through art, craft, and dance. The supervisor spoke to the music and mathematics teachers who both showed keen interest in assisting the student and he, himself, helped her in one of his areas of expertise.

It was her first year, like many others in the special evening class for students who had not taken up the opportunity of "Universal Education for All" during the day sessions. The supervisor understood the particular need and, as was his wont, strategized and implemented a plan so that students could work on basic subjects, the arts, and a craft/trade. Those who consistently showed interest would be given the opportunity to sit the exams in three years. The supervisor was quite a proactive visionary and nothing deterred him from helping others, particularly the less fortunate. He, indeed, made the system work for the students; he never saw barriers, only hurdles to jump over. He knew their personal histories and he knew how to get necessary help for specific individuals. Some of us, proudly dubbed our school the "Night University" (we deleted the Carib name of 'Koko' for emphasis) as under his guidance and encouragement, we aided many in acquiring the skills they required to improve their competences.

EPISODE 2

TRAINING FOR THE GAME

Victoria, along with six other students of the sixteen on roll, was showing a keen interest in the programme. Victoria was reading and writing better than was anticipated. She evidently had a good background before her mishap. She was re-establishing her forgotten schema and progressed rapidly at each level of the language arts. She gave us such encouragement, always smiling despite her problems that the supervisor soon added literature to her timetable. We were grooming the sextet for the regional examination, and she was certainly our chief dark horse.

Her life at home had also improved; she reported that she still received the occasional punch if she ate more than her apportioned serving, even if it was given to her by the adopted big brother. The lady would scream at both of them. After doing her chores, she would be instructed to "go and study," so she had little choice but to excel. Television viewing was entirely at the lady's discretion. At school, we gave her the necessary encouragement, allowing her to participate in almost every activity we planned, and she always proved to be a willing individual.

Although she was sixteen, she wore designs more suited to ten-year-olds whenever she came to class without her uniform. The lady was the owner of a ladies' apparel boutique in the city and insisted that she, Victoria, should dress "like a child". Her hair was always plaited in true golliwog fashion, which she expressly abhorred, but she dared not alter the lady's styles. She was extremely thin, tall with smooth dark skin, which contrasted starkly with white, even teeth and pale jaundiced eyes. As yet, she was not remarkably attractive; one could perceive though, that she would certainly, like the ugly duckling, metamorphose into the beautiful swan. She had features which when filled out and combined with an attractive hairstyle and appropriate clothes, would add to a striking, desirable presence. However, we, the teachers, were training our girl and we anticipated that the fruit of our labour would certainly make us all happy. It would be the opening of a new door for Victoria, and despite the lady's disposition, she too would be happy to know that she had a hand in the making of a star—from vagrancy to a successful young lady.

Six of our alumni were on the team to Germany—the Caribee Waraos. Like their coach, Ballshaker, we teachers were working hard with our players. They were trying, writing and rewriting, wanting to give up, but holding on because of our promise of a better life and their respect for us, particularly the well-loved supervisor. Victoria was always in the fore, doing twice the amount of work required. Sometimes, the others would be pleading to not have to continue taking notes or writing an assignment, but I would simply refuse to stop until I saw definite signs of exhaustion. The goal was right before me, and like a good forward, I was not going to relent until the ball was firmly lodged in the net; I was prepared to use my entire being to save them. The same pressure was placed on them in other classes. I ensured, however, that my classes were a mixture of fun and laughter with appropriate bouts of comic relief pertinent to classroom activities.

Victoria had the entire class sympathy, which she probably thrived on. I had started giving her vitamin B100, and we, the teachers, were always ready to ensure that she had sufficient to eat, never too much, because at all costs, she had to leave room for the lady's dinner. Victoria loved school and equally loved going to church. She was quietly courteous and obedient. She was ready to play the game of her life; we all silently blessed her.

EPISODE 3

THE IMMINENT HARVEST

She timidly walked into the office, gradually breaking into a smile when she observed that we all wore smiles.

"Sir, miss, I pass!" as her eyes swept through our faces.

"Passed well—three out of five subjects! News to celebrate!" the supervisor happily responded as he rose to shake her hands and give her the expected fatherly hug!

We all hugged her and encouraged her to repeat the two residual subjects. Two other students had passed one subject each and like the others, had fallen one grade below a passing grade in other subject areas. We were all happy because it spoke volumes for teamwork. We had students who for various reasons, had never attended school after having been assigned to a school at age eleven. Apparently, there were no truant officers to ensure that children under the mandatory age of twelve attend school. Such students, once the supervisor became aware of them scattered throughout the community, had been encouraged to join the evening class. The supervisor had the support of the day school principal in the creation of additional classes or as we, the Koko School teachers would say, a school within a school. The principal himself with other committed teachers liaised with the wider community to encourage students and parents to develop positive attitudes towards education. The principal, like us, and indeed the entire country was ecstatic. We had all been on the edge of our seats when the final whistle blew in Germany in the Sweden versus Caribee Waraos' game. Several of the players were graduates of our Football School; they symbolized beacons of hope for many within the community: 0-0! The final outcome, like the results of the six other students, were what others would probably consider as failure. The victory we all celebrated was the reality of having advanced significantly towards our ultimate goal and should not be misconstrued as giving a new meaning to failure. We at the Koko School had two major reasons to celebrate that year! On the football field and in the classroom, it had become increasingly evident that the harvest was imminent.

Suggested Further Readings:

Payne, R. K. (2005). *A framework for understanding poverty*. Highlands, TX: aha!Process, Inc.

CONCLUSION

PERSISTENT SYSTEMIC ISSUES

Can any system in any part of the world address the individual needs of every student? Obviously impossible, from Aristotle's era to the present, philosophers and researchers have pondered on the curricula and the delivery of a connected syllabi in our democratic societies. Teacher interns are eclectically guided but several, after working for a few years, become concerned about the gifted students, the special students (some of whom should not be in the average school), the bullies who sit in the best place possible—in the back row—to avoid the teacher. The children know it, and the teachers know it.

The management of the classroom creates a micro gap, and it affects the delivery of the syllabus, the process, the product, and the praxis. The main focus is to have peaceful delivery to those who are interested and ably concentrated on the assigned task. However, when the gap is great within a small island nation, it forces a reflection of the when and the how of requisite changes within the system. The society is changing rapidly and advancing technologically, but the system apparently is not keeping pace with the requirements of *the children in the back row* and others who in many instances are not suited for the present level of academia.

In more developed societies, there are coordinated interventions by specialists operating within the school system to identify and improve the lives of the socially misplaced, the special and the gifted students. Even without reference to statistical data, the perception that proportionally fewer students in developed countries are exposed to neglect because of the nexus between the institution of school and family may not be completely unfounded. Those societies are aware of the flaws in their system and researchers have been proposing new and/or old modifications to meet the needs of their students—*the back row* included.

This episodic unfolding of relevant capsules from 1956 to 2006 in Caribee and Cruso schools seeks to illustrate a creeping system in need of fundamental restructuring or retrofitting to meet the needs of individuals like *the children in the back row*. Historically, myriad initiatives have been attempted to make sense of the relevant education curricula of the educational institutions from the preschool to the tertiary level. There have been many discourses on green or white papers and education plans between representatives of the Ministry of Education and administrators and or their delegates at various symposia and seminars to explore the notion of best practice. Invariably, contributions from stakeholders are invited only after the technical design has been planned and approved by selected educators who often are no longer in touch with the extant reality of the classroom. Each change of government lays claim to its own indelible brand of change—the top-down model and outside-in being clearly evident. It might be worthwhile to consider emulating our regional neighbour, Little England, where it is understood that education policy never seems to be unduly disrupted by a change of government; the continuity reflects rapid and solid development.

Particularly, at the primary school level the teachers are often unable to restructure students' seating arrangements from the traditional vertical rows to desirable circles or horseshoe settings, depending on the assigned task because of the lack of space for free mobility by both teachers and students. To this date, 2011, many classrooms, particularly at the primary level—the seat of foundation—generally remain overcrowded and are still arranged as they were in 1956. Students sit in rows, classrooms separated by movable blackboards, the rooms are noisily deafening as students and teachers operate in the cacophony of a misplaced learning environment. Additionally, depending on the physical size of the teacher or student, a sidewalk is required between the separated rows of desks. Thus at the extreme poles, the gifted (intellectually brilliant beyond their chronological age group) feel a great sense of boredom, while the specially-abled wallow in fear or low self-esteem and the bullies ignore the teacher from the sanctuary of *the back row.*

Our universities are preparing graduates who could address much of our youths' social issues through the fields of psychology and social work. Currently, interns in the teaching profession are being instructed in the criticality of teamwork. They are also encouraged to develop their technological creativity as strategies for assisting the overall development of children in the system who manifest special needs. However, quantum leaps will become possible when other institutions such as the family and church assume greater systemic roles in bridging the gap for preschoolers, primary, and secondary students. There must be strategies to fine-tune our monitoring or accountability systems to ensure that the vast majority of students benefit from our education system. Our expectation may not extend to every student, but there will certainly be more hope than we have had in the last forty years. Why forty years? Perhaps the response is embedded in our spiraling crime rate perpetrated primarily by citizens who fall within that age group.

The USA, Japan, and the United Kingdom are examples of countries where immigration policy has been deliberately used to import teachers from diverse international/ cultural backgrounds as part of the mandate both to maintain a workable ratio in the classroom and to cater to the needs of ethnic and cultural minorities. Thus, not only is universal education made more attainable for all, but the lives of at-risk students and the specially gifted are potentially more effectively guided and improved as their researchers and administrators continually reassess their unique issues. Such systems constitute fast-tracked attempts at changing the fates of atypical students like the Ixoras, the Johns, the Akeems, the Victorias; not only for the students themselves, but for safer, healthier societies.

In conclusion, as was previously indicated, this part-fictional novel embedded in real settings is an attempt to add to the many voices of educators demanding equity. Reflective teachers who try to reach out to those whom the well-intentioned education policies have left out must be conscious of never forgetting their intrinsic task that could be thwarted as a result of a disconnect among the institutions. The school cannot stand alone. The church, mosque, mandir, temple cannot stand alone. The family should not stand alone.

There are many questions that we could ask concerning atypical students. There is seldom any meaningful response to our individual queries; perhaps collective appeals to those in authority on behalf of the youths may elicit more effective action. This—*a voice for the children in the back row*—is hopefully not just another of the many desperate voices crying disparately in the education wilderness.

Suggested Further Readings:

John-Charles-Baynes, S. (2009, March). *The school climate and its impact upon the self-concept of adolescents in the secondary school system and its relationship to academic achievers.* Paper presented at the Tenth SALISES Annual Conference School Climate and Impact, UWI Cave Hill Campus, Barbados. Abstract retrieved from http://www.cavehill.UWI.edu/salises/conf

Ministry of Education, Trinidad and Tobago. (1993). *Education policy paper (1993-2003): National Task Force of Education (white paper)—Philosophy and educational objectives.* Port of Spain, Republic of Trinidad and Tobago: Ministry of Education.

Pukey, W. W. (1970). *Self-concept and school achievement.* Upper Saddle River, NJ: Prentice Hall.

Tyson, E. (2012). *Progress in politics: Progress in education?* Retrieved from http://Jamaica-gleaner.com/gleaner/20120101/cleisure/cleisure/s.html